"As someone who is grieving, I was deeply moved by Ed Welch's wisdom, compassion, and humility as he explores impactful ways to love those who are in my position. If you are looking for sensitive and practical ways to walk with anyone who is mourning the death of someone they love, this is the book to read."
   Ron Lutz, Pastor Emeritus, New Life Presbyterian Church, Dresher, PA

"This Christ-centered book is a treasure chest of biblical wisdom and practical guidance for becoming a conduit of compassion. Reading it made me want to be more like Jesus. I look forward to seeing how the Holy Spirit uses it to help individuals and churches grow in humility and grace."
   Paul Tautges, Pastor; counselor; author of several books, including *A Small Book for the Hurting Heart: Meditations on Loss, Grief, and Healing*

"Having been a pastor for many decades, I have personally witnessed the lack of sensitivity in the words of folks who think that they are comforting a bereaved person but are actually having the opposite impact. Welch's practical book is exactly what we need as we search for the right words (and actions) to truly comfort others in their time of need. Very helpful to me were his suggestions of words to avoid!"
   Timothy Witmer, Author of *The Shepherd Leader*; emeritus professor of Practical Theology, Westminster Theological Seminary

"This book is a treasure. It does far more than show you how to respond with humility and compassion. Ed reveals how to become the kind of person that suffering people long for—and need. I'm going to do everything I can to make sure that all of our GriefShare leaders know about this powerful book."
   Sam Hodges IV, President, GriefShare

"Just like all of Ed's teaching and resources, this book is beautifully Christ-centered, gospel-driven, and thoroughly practical. It marvelously and helpfully answers the essential question of how to help our friends and family in their suffering. All believers need to grow in how to comfort one another in Christ!"

John C. Kwasny, Executive Ministry Director,
Pear Orchard Presbyterian Church, Ridgeland, MS;
director, One Story Ministries; author

"As I began reading through this great little book, I cringed at memories of unhelpful or untimely words I've heard others speak. But as I continued to read, my disappointment in others morphed into a conviction regarding my own shortcomings. Ed Welch humbly and gently ushered me into the lives of the grieving and showed me both the ways I've lacked compassion and the way forward in love. I am wiser and more seasoned for having read it, and I am eager to get it into the hands of our entire church family."

Scott Mehl, Pastor, Cornerstone Church of
West Los Angeles

"It's all too easy to misunderstand or mishandle people in mourning. In this insightful resource, Ed Welch helps us to consider how to become humble conduits of God's comfort instead of hasty counselors who speak hurtful words. If you want to grow in your ability to speak *with*—not *at*—someone who is suffering grief, this book is for you."

Christine Chappell, Author of *Midnight Mercies*; host,
Hope + Help Podcast, Institute for Biblical Counseling & Discipleship

SOMEONE I KNOW IS GRIEVING

CARING WITH HUMILITY AND COMPASSION

Edward T. Welch

New Growth Press

newgrowthpress.com

New Growth Press, Greensboro, NC 27401
newgrowthpress.com
Copyright © 2023 by Edward T. Welch

All rights reserved. No part of this publication may be reproduced, stored in a retrieval system, or transmitted in any form by any means, electronic, mechanical, photocopy, recording, or otherwise, without the prior permission of the publisher, except as provided by USA copyright law.

Unless otherwise indicated, all Scripture quotations are taken from the The Holy Bible, English Standard Version. ESV® Text Edition: 2016. Copyright © 2001 by Crossway Bibles, a publishing ministry of Good News Publishers.

Scripture quotations marked NIV are taken from the Holy Bible, New International Version®, NIV® Copyright © 1973, 1978, 1984, 2011 by Biblica, Inc.® Used by permission of Zondervan. All rights reserved worldwide.

Cover Design: Studio Gearbox, studiogearbox.com
Interior Typesetting and eBook: Lisa Parnell, lparnellbookservices.com

ISBN: 978-1-64507-373-4 (Print)
ISBN: 978-1-64507-374-1 (eBook)

Library of Congress Cataloging-in-Publication Data
Names: Welch, Edward T., 1953- author.
Title: Someone I know is grieving : caring with humility and compassion / Edward T. Welch.
Description: Greensboro, NC : New Growth Press, [2023] | Series: Ask the Christian counselor | Includes bibliographical references. | Summary: "Learn to approach those who are grieving with the same compassion and humility that Jesus shows us, listening well and providing practical support"-- Provided by publisher.
Identifiers: LCCN 2023017819 (print) | LCCN 2023017820 (ebook) | ISBN 9781645073734 (Print) | ISBN 9781645073741 (e-book)
Subjects: LCSH: Grief--Religious aspects--Christianity. | Compassion--Religious aspects--Christianity. | Consolation.
Classification: LCC BV4905.3 .W3795 2023 (print) | LCC BV4905.3 (ebook) | DDC 248.8/6--dc23/eng/20230614
LC record available at https://lccn.loc.gov/2023017819
LC ebook record available at https://lccn.loc.gov/2023017820

Printed in India

31 30 29 28 27 26 25 24   4 5 6 7 8

To Paul Tautges,
a humble and compassionate pastor.

CONTENTS

Chapter 1: Responding Wisely to Suffering 1

Chapter 2: Hear More from Christ Our Wisdom....... 15

Chapter 3: Care Shaped by Compassion 31

Chapter 4: Care Shaped by Humility........................... 45

Resources 67

Endnotes 69

Chapter 1

RESPONDING WISELY TO SUFFERING

*My joy is gone; grief is upon me;
my heart is sick within me. (Jeremiah 8:18)*

Have you ever been open with your own troubles, and then you were hurt even more by someone's response?

Ask that question of *anyone*—they still remember those words.

"I confided in my mother about being sad that I could not have more children. She said, 'At least you have one.'"

"I am in a small group at my church, and the men meet once a month. A few months ago I mentioned that this has been the hardest season of my life . . . and no one has said a word."

"My ten-year-old son was playing soccer at recess with some of the older boys when one of them started calling my son names and then tripped him while they were playing. My son was left in tears from both the humiliation and the fall. When I mentioned this to a neighbor, she talked about how this is the way boys get a thicker skin."

A teenage girl said, "I don't talk about hard things with my friends anymore because they will either tell other people or they talk about *their* hard things."

We all have similar stories, and we have most likely contributed to these stories.

Yet there are other stories we could tell too. Have you ever been open with your own pain and someone said just the right thing?

"This is horrible. I am so sorry."

"I am so sorry. You really loved your father. Could you tell me more about him?"

"That is overwhelming. Please, tell me what happened."

[After receiving a text] "I'm on my way."

As you look back, you understand that these were gifts from God himself as his people functioned on his behalf.

Helpful words draw us together. Friends both share their hearts with others and hear the hearts of others. Know and be known—that is an essential feature of our humanity.

Unhelpful words distance us from each other. In response, we keep our misery to ourselves rather than allow a community to bear it with us. We learned a lesson: keep your sorrows to yourself.

WE HAVE A PROBLEM

Let's agree that we have a problem. At our best, we would like to go through life without hurting other people. We especially don't want to hurt those who are already hurt. But we do. Though we can have the best of intentions, we have all said unhelpful or hurtful words to suffering people, or, perhaps even worse, we said nothing at all. When grieving people most need words that encourage, we can be at our most inept. Suffering is isolating in itself; insensitive words intensify it even while we know that the Spirit has been given to bring us as one. All this dulls our display of the "God of all comfort" (2 Corinthians 1:3). With this in mind, our project is about wisdom. Wisdom is about God-given life skills. Among those skills are words that help the hurting, and those words can even be beautiful to the one who receives them. "A word fitly spoken is like apples of gold in a setting of silver" (Proverbs 25:11).

The goal of what follows is simple: to care very well for those who suffer; to bring life to those who are hurting. As we grow in this goal, the body of Christ will be drawn both toward Jesus and toward each other.

Imagine a church community in which you share your heart with someone and their words or deeds bring comfort.

Imagine being in a small group. You carry the weight of an anniversary of a loved one's death, but you decide to say nothing about it because you don't want to complain or bring attention to yourself. Then someone notices that you are not quite right. Soon, you are pouring out your heart, and the person cries along with you.

Imagine a church community in which you are open with your struggles and people pray for you. A week later they track you down, let you know how they are still praying for you, tell you what Scripture they are actually praying, and ask if there is another way they should pray.

The goal is simple; the consequences in a community are profound. If you and a few others are inspired to grow in the way you care for those in pain (and all of us live with many troubles), those you care for will pass on that care to others, and your community will arrive at a tipping point where love is more obvious, people are joined together, and the name of Jesus is honored.

And the community you influence can reach beyond the church. Most of us who have put our faith in Jesus want to represent Jesus well to the world around us, and most of us believe that we fall far short of doing that well. We think of what we could have said about Christ *after* a conversation. We have relationships in which we are timid to talk about Jesus. Now consider the people you speak to during the week whose lives are especially difficult. A friend, coworker, neighbor, or staff at a store or restaurant. If you know of a particular burden in their lives, you have already been let into their hearts.

Now compassion can lead the way. You can say *something* about those hardships.

"I've been thinking about you. I am so sorry."

"My husband and I believe that God hears and he is filled with compassion, so we have been praying for you."

Compassion is in high demand all around us, and most people receive very little. When given, it brings people together and sets us on a path that leads toward Jesus.

YOUR RESPONSE TO YOUR OWN SUFFERING

Think of the work ahead as a group project—like a Wikipedia article—in which we all learn and we all contribute. Everyone comes to this task with some experience already. We have some idea of words that have been helpful for us. Let's bring that experience and then build on it. Sprinkled throughout this book are bulleted, italicized questions for discussion and reflection in italics. Take the time to work through them on your own and with others.

For now, start by considering how you respond to your *own* troubles and grief. How you respond will shape how you help others. Different personalities respond to suffering in different ways—God does not prescribe a formula we must follow. But one thing is clear: in God's kingdom—that is, in his house—he invites us to talk to him and to others.

This is how human beings are intended to live. Suffering is not something that we keep to ourselves.

Do you speak with other people about your own grief?

As you care well for those you love, you invite them to open their hearts. It is difficult to care when the other person is not known. Now turn this principle back to yourself. Are *you* willing to speak openly when your life is hard? Do you ask for help? As a general rule, we ask others to do what we have already done. It would be odd if you valued openness for other people but you have not practiced it yourself. Before long you would sound like a teacher more than a friend, and we all know that such a role is not ideal, especially in our initial attempts to care for people. Here again, we discover that life in God's kingdom is different from what we might expect: it is not so much the expert who is most helpful to others, but it is needy people that God uses. And needy, of course, is not easy.

We prefer to project competence rather than ask for help. Men are particularly hesitant here. We might admire other people who can be open with their sufferings, but our pride leaves us silent. When we acknowledge our own hardships we admit that we are weak in ourselves, and, of course, we are not keen to state the obvious. Though weakness is the essence of faith, we can be reluctant to say that daily life is beyond our own capacities. With this in mind, both our compassion *and* humility will become prominent in what is ahead.

There are other stumbling blocks to our openness too. Perhaps we thought that the culture of God's house was not much different from the world, in which people live in their own worlds with their silent burdens. Though the Psalms are proof of his enthusiasm for us to speak to him, it is still hard to believe. For me personally, one of the hardest things to believe is that God actually desires to be present and close to his people, and, from that place, he delights to hear us and bless us.

- *Is it hard for you to believe that God wants you to speak openly to him? What are the roadblocks for you in being open with God and others?*

Even our pride or lack of knowledge does not tell the whole story. We can also be reserved because other people have not invited us to speak and have not cared when we do. Our own pasts can add to our silence. We only need one brush with someone's disdain for weakness.

"Well, life is hard."

"You should be thankful that it wasn't worse."

Or perhaps we shared our pain with someone who simply changed the subject. The disinterest of others will certainly teach us that life is safer when we keep our troubles to ourselves.

When silent, we appear in control and self-sufficient, but the truth is that we are not actually in control or independent, and we truly need God and the help of others. Anything different is to go against the grain of the human condition and is unsustainable. Such a lifestyle has consequences. For one, we become more isolated, and *that* intensifies our suffering.

- *How have other people contributed to your silence?*

- *What have they said or not said that was hard or hurtful?*

- *Was there ever a moment in which you decided that you would not share your heart again?*

Do you put your trust in other people?

Now go one step deeper. The answer is not only that we become more open with others and ask for their help. We always look for a refuge when life is beyond our ability to manage. That refuge could be work, activities, entertainment, pornography, food, or drugs. Or—and this is our favorite refuge—it could be other people. We can be sure it will be in something.

Do you speak openly of your suffering to other people but not to the Lord? When we have good friends and confidants, we naturally speak to them about the persistent hardships of life. That is good and right, unless our vulnerability stops there. Scripture warns us that our hearts are at risk from trusting in people rather than the Lord (Jeremiah 17:5–7). One of those ways we can trust in people is by pouring our hearts out to them yet being silent before the God of power and love whose "ears are attentive" to our cries (Psalm 34:15). Even our sins cannot separate us from his love. If we are slow to speak from our heart to the Lord, we are finding refuge somewhere else.

- *Are other people your refuge? This doesn't mean that you should avoid talking to them. It means that you aim to talk to Jesus more.*

Do you speak to the Lord when hardships overtake you?

Your words could be as simple as, "Jesus, help."

They could be the same words you speak to a friend: "This week has been so hard. I feel like death itself is close. I feel like I am coming undone."

They could be words borrowed from a psalm or a hymn.

Do you speak to him when troubles overtake you? Do you speak to him first or only after you have exhausted most other forms of help and solace?

Yes, our goal of wanting to care well for others gets personal—it's about you before the Lord. This, of course, is the tradition in God's house. Before we invite others to speak from their hearts, we respond to his plea to "pour out your hearts to him, for God is our refuge" (Psalm 62:8 NIV). He is "our ever-present help in trouble." We begin with our own neediness. As we learn of our own need before God and others, this becomes the primary qualification for helping others in need.

- *Take time to speak to the Lord about what has been hard. Practice doing that now. The basic rule is this: you speak to him knowing that he is the one who formed the ear because he hears.*

How have other people blessed you when your life has been hard?

Even if we are slow to speak openly about our troubles, we *have* spoken, at some point, to someone. We naturally want to speak to others about the wonderful things of life and the painful things. We have confided in others, and sometimes it went well. What have you learned from people who have encouraged your own heart?

- *Who are your safe and trustworthy people?*

- *What makes them trusted stewards of your troubles?*

- *What have they said or done that has been good for your soul?*

Our wisdom project has begun, and we can gather at least three insights. First, if we are to offer healing words, we must have heard those words from Christ for our own hearts. Our care for others will depend on us settling into God's house and receiving his comfort.

Second, we understand why so many people have decided to keep their troubles to themselves. Like us, they have been hurt by foolish comments. Why would they be open again? But we also know this: since we were designed to be an interdependent and open people, that design will compel us to violate any vows of silence and, once again, share our hearts with someone who seems to care. In other words, we *want* to share our troubles. A trace of compassion is enough to invite them out.

Third, we already have experience in hearing both helpful and unhelpful words. We want those experiences to warn us and guide us.

- *How would you summarize the most important insights you have for helping others when they are hurting?*

Chapter 2

HEAR MORE FROM CHRIST OUR WISDOM

From here we could move directly into a list of what to do and what not to do, but not yet. The wisdom we already have assures us that our capacity to build up those who are suffering is dependent on a deeper wisdom, which is to know and rest in Jesus. This project is a quest for more wisdom, and wisdom is founded "in Christ Jesus, who has become for us wisdom from God" (1 Corinthians 1:30 NIV). So we will linger over how Christ is our wisdom, who reshapes our own hearts with love and humility, *then* we will gather new skills and specific words that can be helpful for others.

CHRIST IS OUR WISDOM

The apostle Paul reminds us that *Christ* is our wisdom because we too often rely on *our* wisdom, which for us means that we trust in our own skills to help others. Instead, God chooses ordinary people like ourselves, who usually feel inadequate, and he equips them to love others in the name of Jesus in such a way that we are actually helpful. In this section of Scripture, the wisdom God gives us in Christ is identified as "our righteousness, holiness and redemption" (1 Corinthians 1:30 NIV). All this is God's doing in you. He has brought you *in* Christ Jesus.

Robert Gundry describes being brought into Christ in this way: "To be in Christ Jesus is for God to relate to you as he relates to him [Christ], because so far as God is concerned you've been incorporated into him."[1] That is why you have the wisdom of God. You have true wisdom because you have Christ, and in him you have righteousness, holiness, and redemption.

Righteousness is your assurance that he has declared you righteous because you are joined to his righteousness. Now you stand with him—you *rest* in him—when he comes to judge what is wrong and to make things right. Because of his righteousness, you can be sure he will be faithful to you and misery will not have the last word.

Holiness is his cleansing you from sin *and* from the sinful acts done against you. Both of these leave us unpresentable and have the power to distance us from other people and God. But God will have none of that. His mission is to bring us close to himself by cleansing us, making us holy, and setting us apart for his service. This is why you can be sure he will use you as you care for others. You are his, and you function as his representative to the world.

Redemption is how he has rescued you from the slavery of sin and bondage to death and the devil. You are now liberated and free people, no longer ruled by the ways of death. This means that you can take a stand against sin and lies rather than be powerless before them, and you can be sure that your sins and struggles will not disqualify you from speaking of redemption to those around you. All this expresses his love and gives you even more confidence that you can speak from your heart to him.

These three ground your wise care for others in the wisdom of Christ. At the heart of this wisdom is that nothing can separate us from the love of Christ or from his power that comforts and gives hope.

Here are some things to remember about growing in wise care for others:

1. Wisdom is found in dependence on Christ. We remember that our caring skills do not proceed merely by learning new techniques. Instead, they are grounded in our faith in Jesus rather than in self-confidence. Our skills grow as we talk with him and ask him for wisdom and love.
2. Wisdom is confident in the love of Christ. How can we speak of God's love and fellowship with us in our

misery when we think that his love is in response to our obedience? God's love, however, is expressed in his righteousness, holiness, and redemption. This is what we need in the midst of our own heartaches. God has pursued us when we were not pursuing him, and he brought us to himself, never to let us go. Immanuel—God with us—is God's primary way of bringing us hope and comfort. He loves us because he is love, not because we are lovable. How has that comfort broken into your own heart?
3. Wisdom, rooted in God's love for us, begins to look ahead with hope. We are people who wait, but with our righteousness, holiness, and redemption tucked away in him, we wait with hope rather than dread. Every human story is surrounded by pain, yet the story told by wisdom is that pain will be banished, and that makes all the difference.

One of the radical features of the church is that this wisdom is distributed to us all. We *all* do the work of ministry, which includes our caring for the hearts of sufferings saints. Whereas the Old Testament ministry was accomplished by the priests with assistance from prophets, today, in this age of the

Spirit, we are all priests before God and each other. That is what happens when we are in Christ. We do "the work of ministry, for building up the body of Christ" (Ephesians 4:12). Not surprisingly, this calling is done "with all humility . . . bearing with one another in love (Ephesians 4:2). The feature of love that takes the lead? Compassion.

THE WAY OF COMPASSION

When one of my daughters was three years old, our extended family gathered for a large reunion. At some point, my daughter had a mishap that ended in tears, and she was on the lookout for someone to comfort her. As she walked through a room of adults, Uncle John rescued her. He picked her up and said, "Sweetie, I am so sorry. Is there anything I can do to help?" Compassion, of course, makes a difference. She was comforted. Tears ceased. From that moment on Uncle John became her go-to person for all things tragic. He loved her, she loved him back, and I loved him for loving her.

Compassion means that you love the person and are affected by his or her hardships, no matter how transient those hardships might be. They leave their mark. You remember them and are changed by them. Such a response takes you into the very heart of God, who chooses to place compassion at the forefront of how we know him.

To an unlikely and unruly group of people, he revealed himself as, "The Lord, the Lord, the compassionate and gracious God" (Exodus 34:6 NIV). Later, after generations of his people rejected him, he proclaimed, "My heart is changed within me; all my compassion is aroused" (Hosea 11:8 NIV). His compassion is so prominent that it would not be dissuaded even by betrayal. So we expect compassion to be on full display when God comes in the flesh.

Jesus was, indeed, moved by the misery that surrounded him. His compassion was certainly aroused. He searched out the leper, the lame, a woman shamed by her bleeding, a woman rejected because of her reputation, and the father whose daughter had just died. Compassion guided his ministry. When he planned to rest with his disciples, he was met by thousands of followers who had run to find him. His response to this change of plans? "He had compassion on them, because they were like sheep without a shepherd" (Mark 6:34). When he told the story of the prodigal son, his point was clear: the heart of God is his compassion. As he saw his son approaching, the father "felt compassion, and ran and embraced him and kissed him" (Luke 15:20).

As the writers of the New Testament epistles reflect upon Jesus and interpret what he did, the writer of Hebrews seizes upon compassion. He identifies Jesus as our high priest. Here the divine and human meet in the One who experienced the worst of human misery and truly understands our own. His priesthood changes everything. "We do not have a high priest who is unable to sympathize with our weaknesses, but one who in every respect has been tempted as we are, yet without sin" (Hebrews 4:15).

To offer compassion, we start by receiving it. Helping skills are built upon truly knowing the compassion of your High Priest toward you. As a way to assess yourself, remember that simple test: Do you cry out to the Lord when your troubles accumulate? We naturally seek out another compassionate person when life is especially hard. If we don't have such a person, our troubles might be expressed to an unsuspecting neighbor or even the supermarket cashier. But do you also draw near to Jesus? The writer of Hebrews invites you to do so. "Let us then with confidence draw near to the throne of grace, that we may receive mercy and find grace to help in time of need" (Hebrews 4:16). When you take Jesus up on his offer of mercy and compassion, you are beginning to understand how things are done in his house.

- *You speak to him more often, with more confidence and boldness.*
- *You notice more of the sufferings of others.*
- *You pray that other sufferers would know the comfort of Jesus, and you ask them to pray with you.*

So enter into the compassion of Christ, and pray that you would know it more.

- *Compassion is what you expect of the Lord when you understand that he is committed to drawing us near to himself.*
- *Reflect on one time when you received compassion from another person. How did that affect you?*

- *Now look more closely at that person. You will see an ambassador of Christ to you. God typically uses people as his body on earth. How does that help you see Christ more clearly in your daily life?*

- *How would you describe or define compassion?*

- *Do you have a favorite passage from Scripture that assures you of God's compassion for you in your suffering? If not, ask your pastor or another wise Christian for verses and stories you can make your own.*

- *Talk about this with friends.*

Compassion will be expressed differently in each of us. For some of us it will be expressed in tears and strong emotions. For others it will be less visceral and intense. No matter how strong or subdued your emotions might run, compassion is a gift from God, which means you can pray to know more of the compassion of Christ. His compassion for you will be the growth of your compassion for others. Then your growing, compassionate love will keep you from hurtful words and be the creative source for inventing apt ways to love a grieving person.

THE WAY OF HUMILITY

You noticed that the apostle Paul reminds us that care is given with patient, compassionate love *and* "with all humility" (Ephesians 4:2). Humility, like compassion, begins with Christ our wisdom. He chose to come to us as the suffering servant, lower, dependent on his Father, and empowered by the Spirit.

For us, the wisdom of Christ comes from humble listening to God's words. We are creatures and he is our Creator. Our lives are dependent on him alone. He is the maker of heaven and earth and we need him.

What do we need from him? Many things. *Everything*. Among them, to know that we do not have all the answers. To know we are less skillful in our care for other people than we might think. To know sin remains active in our hearts, and sin is known by its pride and independence. We need humility.

One of the ways pride contaminates all our relationships is that we think we are right, or at least more right than the people around us. When this pride shows itself in our care for each other, it looks like this: we give advice.

We seem to have a near-incurable instinct. We believe that suffering needs an answer. Our job is to dispense expert advice to the person in pain, solve the problem, and then move on to the next person, like a busy physician who dispenses prescriptions for ailing patients.

A father wrote a letter with some very difficult news to his church. His teenage daughter had been diagnosed with cancer. She was already under the care of one of the finest medical centers in the country and the medical team had agreed on a course of treatment with cautious optimism.

He made two requests. First, he asked for prayer—for his family to see more of Jesus during this difficult time. Second, he asked the church *not* to send the family any articles on medical treatments or any cures for their daughter. He said that she was under fine medical care, and the family simply could not sift through more treatment options. Well-intended advice would be a burden rather than a blessing.

The advice, of course, began pouring in the next morning. After a month he wrote another letter to the church and asked the congregation to stop, and again, the advice only increased. We can understand why the father decided to no longer share his family's burden with the congregation. An occasion which could make the congregation a larger family sadly became one in which the father and his immediate family confided only in a few trusted friends. Yes, we can understand that when someone believes they have found the one effective treatment for all cancers, then that person would feel obligated to pass the treatment to others. It *seems* loving. Humility, however, listens. Humility is also reluctant to stand in judgment over medical professionals who have invested their entire adult lives into learning about the disease and its treatments.

There are times when a family asks people *not* to visit someone with a chronic illness, and we might wonder if we should be ruled by the principle that our love should pursue people and not leave them to their isolation. Perhaps we should visit anyway? We also might think we are among the inner circle—the sick person's favorite—and we are the exceptions to the ban. Humility, however, listens. If a family asks us to stay away for a season, that family will also identify ways we can bless the sick person. If they have not, then we can ask. One of the ways we hurt suffering people is that we think we know best what they really need. The humble alternative is that we ask them simple questions.

- "Could you help me to understand something about your pain and how it affects your daily life?"
- "What do you think would be most helpful for you?"

If the person has no idea what would be helpful, we pray, together, to "the Father of mercies and God of all comfort, who comforts us in all our affliction" (2 Corinthians 1:3–4).

Humility strikes an unusual balance in that we have a growing awareness of our own need and capacity to do harm, and we have increased confidence in God's strength and his plan to mature us and make us fruitful (John 15:1–9).

Here is a good place to pause. We know that we are on the path of wisdom when we ask for it. "If any of you lacks wisdom, let him ask God, who gives generously to all without reproach, and it will be given him" (James 1:5). Wisdom needs God and listens to him.

- *Confession of need and sin is more pleasant and hopeful than it first appears. First, it confronts reality. We are sinners who need Jesus. Second, Jesus has said that the physician comes only to those who are sick (Luke 5:31). Confession of need, therefore, is the shortcut to knowing his closeness and care. So confess your daily need for Jesus. Be specific. What do you need? Ask him for wisdom in how you love other people.*

This humility then carries into our everyday relationships and changes how we care for each other. Instead of being the teacher, we walk together with others as we humbly listen to the Lord.

- *How can humility be a new asset for you in the way you respond to the grief of other people? Think first about how humility can provide new ways to bless your family—parents, siblings, children.*

- *If you are convicted about how you did not care for a family member, take time to actually say that and confess your lack of love. Ask the person what was helpful or what could have been helpful.*

Since humility listens and wants to learn, ask friends what other people did that helped them in their own times of hardship. Ask them what did not help. Let those answers make you wiser.

Wisdom is first humility before God. We are creatures and he is our Creator. Our lives are dependent on him alone. As we grow in it, humility will protect us from so many hurtful comments, especially as it is wrapped in love. Wise care grows out of the partnership of humility and love.

Chapter 3

CARE SHAPED BY COMPASSION

Now we are ready to put this into action in the way we care for each other. You can easily find dozens of lists of what *to* say and what *not* to say to grieving people. I will identify some of the common features of these lists; we certainly want to learn from and contribute to them. But we need more than that. Scripture takes us beyond lists. It reshapes our hearts with compassion and humility so that we can invent new ways to bless.

Love and compassion want to know the other person. No broad brushstrokes or brief summary. When love has time, it wants details.

"Please, tell me more."

We can care for each other from two different vantage points: from eyes that look through the lens of a camera, or from ears that hear the heart.

A camera watches events. It answers questions such as these: What happened? What did he say?

What did she say? What did you say? What did you do?

I knew a man in his mid-thirties who was planning to end a dating relationship with a woman his age. The relationship had seemed promising. He clearly admired the woman and she him. His concerns were about her parents. Parents intrude and can be hard to please, but he was not dating the parents so I didn't understand how they could control his decision.

Love is interested in the details, so I asked, "How do they interfere?"

"They decide when I can see her, they impose curfews when we are together, and they call her when they worry, which happens every day. She always takes the calls. She has lived on her own for over a decade, and she has not been able to talk to her parents about these things. She wants to, but it is easier to do what they say than deal with their frenzied reactions."

The details were important. My compassion was aroused, and I suddenly appreciated his patience and gentleness.

Yet the vantage point of the heart is deeper. The heart is the real person—the joys, the pain, the desires that always hear "not yet," the growth and struggles in following Jesus. The heart is handled with particular care, and you might have to show yourself trustworthy before someone shares it.

Sometimes you are trustworthy if you simply show genuine interest.

"How are *you*?"

"It's been six months since the funeral. How can I pray?" When you remember, your interest and care are unmistakable.

Or how about this: "Do you still miss your pet?" God does not judge between big losses and smaller ones. His compassion responds to your present grief, even if you think you should be over something.

Compassion knows that our emotions can be complex. We can enjoy others and laugh, but that isn't the entire story. "Even in laughter the heart may ache, and the end of joy may be grief" (Proverbs 14:13). So a composed or happy countenance is not enough to make you think all is well. There is a gentle pursuit in love that wants to truly know the suffering person. It is in that wise and gentle pursuit that suffering people are brought out of their isolation.

The book of Proverbs makes this observation. "The heart knows its own bitterness, and no stranger shares its joy" (Proverbs 14:10). This is not a reason to give up because we can never break through the armor of misery. It is an invitation for love to know more, and since that journey is beyond our abilities, we pray for wisdom and love.

WAYS TO EXTEND A COMPASSIONATE INVITATION

Say something.

Let's say that someone you care for has gone through a significant loss, and you heard it from someone else. The loss is not a secret. You simply were not the first to hear about it. For example, you learn that someone's child has recently been diagnosed with a dangerous disease. Your heart is heavy from the news. Your compassion is aroused. Too often, that is as far as compassion goes. You speak about the tragedy with others, you pray for the family, but you don't say anything to the family members. Perhaps you are worried that whatever you say will add to the family's burdens.

Then you remember the compassion of God. He pursues you. He doesn't wait for you to come to him. He pursues you as your high priest who understands your pain and speaks to you. His house is filled with words.

When your compassion is aroused, say something. *Something.* What happened is too important for you to remain silent. Suffering isolates, and our silence isolates even more. Compassionate words draw sufferers into fellowship.

Words, however, can be elusive when the suffering of another person is overwhelming. If you are without words, you might default back toward silence and be tempted to say nothing. This, however, is not okay in God's house. We are building a house together where many good words are spoken. The day begins with "The Lord bless you . . ." (Numbers 6:24–27), and it ends with the same words. Between those benedictions are more personal blessings that suit specific situations. There are invitations galore. God invites us to speak about painful matters and to speak about him. Likewise, you invite those around you to do the same. The kingdom of God is far from silent, so we commit ourselves to finding good words.

Do you share in the person's sorrow? Speak honest and simple words, "You have been on my heart. I am so sorry for you and your family." If not these words, pray and consider what words are on your heart. Ask trustworthy people if they are appropriate. If you still have no words, ask for help. But *say something*.

Avoid questions at first. "How are you?" is a very good question *before* the onset of grief, but usually a thoughtless one in the midst of it. If the grief is public, you already know that the person is undone. But say something, write something, or send a card that says something.

- *Notice that humility has snuck in—you ask for help. Wise care for other people is a gift from God that he freely gives to those who seek it. It is not the domain of those who seem to have the right word for every occasion. Who can you say something to today? Who can you ask for help in knowing what to say?*

Never start a sentence with "At least . . ."

Compassion invites words. But if your words are poorly chosen, they put an end to conversations. "At least" kills conversations.

"At least you still have your health."
"At least no one else died."
"At least she is in a better place."
"At least her suffering is over."

Even if the grieving person uses those words—such as "at least my husband is with the Lord"—we do not use them. No one has ever responded to such words with, "Thank you. I never thought of that. I feel better now." When these words are well-intentioned, perhaps we hope to encourage thankfulness "in all things."[2] But there is no version of "at least" in God's house. It suggests that God divvies out his compassion according to some predetermined scale that identifies some suffering as deserving of less compassion than other suffering. In this scheme, God reserves his limited store of compassion for only the worthiest candidates, and this bereaved person is not among them. That is a destructive lie.

The danger of any attempt to minimize suffering is that grieving people no longer feel justified to pour out their hearts to the Lord. Jesus counters this lie as our sympathetic High Priest, and he invites us to come to him with everything that is important to us. So "let us then with confidence draw near." God forbid that we would lessen someone's confidence or direct someone away from coming to him.

- *Wisdom considers the fruit of our words. Are there people who have been through deep waters you can ask, "What was helpful, and what was unhelpful?" They will probably mention any attempt to minimize suffering as near the top of the list of unhelpful comments.*

Another way you can discern what is helpful is in how people respond. If they respond with more open sharing of their own hearts, you probably spoke helpful words. If they are relatively silent, your words did not invite.

Avoid stories about you.

We all share stories about ourselves. That is a part of everyday conversation that can be engaging and draw people together. We want to know others *and* be known. We also want to be wise. If we notice that our stories are taking more space than those of other people, we shift to draw out *their* stories. That is a wise principle in all our conversations. During times of other people's suffering, we are even more careful. As a general rule, compassion would lead us to not only shift to their stories—it would also suggest that there are times when we do not add in our personal stories at all.

Perhaps you have noticed that so many conversations begin with someone telling a story, and then the other person shares a similar story, which might one-up the preceding story.

> "Working from home has become more difficult. There are more distractions, more noise, more interruptions. Today I left a meeting to answer a knock on the door, which turned out to be a person selling replacement windows."

"Yeah, I know what you mean. You wouldn't believe what happened to me today . . ."

One-upping another person's story can kill conversations. The message is clear: *I am not interested in what you have to say.*

What about the place of our personal stories in our care for those in pain?

A friend revealed that she was just laid off and was afraid because she had little financial reserve. What if your response was to say, "I remember when I lost a job and had no idea how I would pay rent. But God gave me a job a week later that was even better."

We attempt to offer understanding or solidarity and hope to a grieving person, and that intent is a good one. But the words are unhelpful.

- *Why do you think these words would be unhelpful?*

- *What would have been better?*

A more severe version is when we try to show compassion with an analogous personal story and the other person becomes the one showing compassion to *us*.

Have you found such stories helpful when you were in pain? Perhaps. But there will be a time for them later. Even if you are persuaded that your story could help, do not deflect the conversation to you. You can find better ways to offer compassion and understanding.

Follow them.

Compassion places the interests of the other person on your heart. This means you give them room to talk, and you listen for what is most important to them. You could put it this way: follow what they feel most strongly, and follow what they repeat.

A mother lost her adult son in a car accident. In her grief, she tells stories about him. Those memories are important to her. To follow her lead, listen for

Care Shaped by Compassion

the reflected beauty of God in her son, whether the deceased son was a follower of Jesus or not.

"A follower of Jesus or not" opens a complex subject. As a general rule, you will not be helpful to someone who has just lost a loved one if you ask about the state of the deceased person's soul. Instead, enjoy whatever you hear that is good.

Listen for what is good and human in the best sense—the son's interests, kindness, gentleness, and love. Value his achievements. And when you are moved by what you hear, you might say, "That is a beautiful story. Thank you for letting me know him a little better." If you knew her son, you could share a story of your own.

Follow what is on the grieving person's heart. When they talk freely, where do they go? To the past, the future, fear, hope, despair? Follow them.

A woman was speaking about the loss of her husband. When she had room to speak, she did not end with grief. She was thankful for the years she had with him and believed he was alive with Jesus. Instead, she was overwhelmed by the practical matters of life—bills, taxes, leaky faucets, car maintenance, and limited finances. She was afraid. Then our love and compassion take a different course. We would review the bills with her, or ask deacons in the church to assist her.

If you don't know what is of most concern, ask a question:

> "Where has your mind been going as you have had to live with such grief?"
>
> "Could you say a little bit about how your nights have been?"
>
> "Could you give me one thing to pray for?"

Such questions can give you access to what is especially important.

Do something, be creative.

Compassion acts. It texts, sends cards, calls, meets for coffee, and creatively considers ways to serve and help. It *does not* say, "Please, if you need anything, call me." They won't call. Your words may be heartfelt, but they put the initiative on the grieving person.

I was listening to a man reflect on his hard bout with cancer and the many days when he could barely move because he was weakened by the treatments. He was well-known and well-loved. People took initiative in many ways, but one stood out. As he remembered this particular person, he began to cry. A neighbor would bring over his mower and care for the lawn so well that it looked as though it was done by a professional landscaper. It was simple, creative compassion that wanted to *do* something, and it was a gift never forgotten.

Here are other ways to act:

- "I'd like to bring dinner over tomorrow."

- "Can I walk the dog?"
- "How about if I pick up your kids and take them to the park?"
- "Would it be more helpful if I stayed with the kids tomorrow afternoon or brought you a meal?"
- "Can I clean your house for you?" (Granted this would have to be a close friend or family member.)

Ask the Spirit to guide you and then ask around. Talk to the grieving person's friends and join together in a way to surprise and serve. (The *surprise* is that you are thinking intently about the other person. The surprise is *not* that you show up unannounced, unless you are certain that it blesses the grieving person and the person confirms that it was a blessing.)

If you have a thought about something you could do, don't ignore it. That is the Spirit at work. Compassion generates ideas on how to serve others.

Remember.

Compassion also means the other person is etched on your heart—you remember them.

After the loss of a loved one, the grieving person experiences a flurry of concern that extends a few days beyond the funeral and then fades away. As everyone gets back to their routines, the grieving person begins to feel the fuller weight of loss and isolation. Those with compassion, however, remember.

> "I wanted to let you know that I was thinking of you and prayed for you this morning. I prayed for you because I know that this is the anniversary of your wife's death, and I am still so sorry for your loss. I miss her."

This note reminded the widower that he was not alone. A community remembered her, and the person who wrote the note—like the neighbor who mowed the lawn—would become a friend.

When someone experiences grief, there are two constants:

1. Grief persists. As time goes on, it can be accompanied by pleasures and the matters of daily life, but still, grief persists.
2. Those who mourn are blessed by simple and small acts of compassion: being remembered at anniversaries and holidays, or being asked if a particular illustration during the sermon was hard to hear. Such small words and actions are received by a weary soul as refreshing waters.

The skill you bring to your care depends on compassion.

Chapter 4

CARE SHAPED BY HUMILITY

Compassion partners with humility. Humility is dependence on God that expresses itself in a desire to serve others. For us, humility knows its creaturely limits and persuades you that your comforting skills need work. You don't always know what is helpful to say or do, and you can't fully understand another person's pain. But you *are* confident in these truths: Jesus hears you because he has forgiven sins once and for all and nothing separates you from him. You will learn and grow. The Spirit will help you.

Humility, of course, was embodied by Jesus. Just watch him serve. The image of Jesus etched on our minds is when he washed the disciples' feet (John 13). He, our King and Savior, bowed down to serve others. Then listen to his words. He is our high priest whose words "deal gently" with us (Hebrews 5:2). He identifies himself as "gentle and lowly" (Matthew 11:29). Paul imitated this gentleness, which he described as the way a nursing mother cares for her young child (1 Thessalonians 2:7). Gentleness is humility's tone. In Jesus, it is expressed through his words that heal and are inevitably kinder than what you expect.

HOW TO HUMBLY CARE FOR OTHERS

Pray.

Humility opens a world of possibilities. You can ask close friends of the hurting person what might be helpful to say or do. You can read Nancy Guthrie's book, *What Grieving People Wish You Knew about What Really Helps*.[3] Most importantly, humility leads you to pray—"Lord, teach me. Help me. Teach me to love and to say words that build up." We pray for ourselves, and we pray for the person in pain. Prayer acknowledges that only God can reach a grieving heart.

For grieving friends who have put their trust in Jesus, ask them, "What is one way I can pray?" And for people who have not yet trusted in Jesus, you can make the same offer. Even those decidedly uninterested in God are generally grateful to be prayed for when their world falls apart.

- *Ask how you can pray. That is the way of humility. But since love has most likely already prompted you to pray, what*

Care Shaped by Humility

Scripture might you already be praying? What are some of the promises of God that you could pray? (A few are mentioned up ahead.)

I met with a husband and wife. He was an avowed atheist unhappily married to a Christian woman. But he committed himself to work on the relationship and a new vision for loving his wife. He had a glimpse of servant-love. A few years later he called and asked if we could meet. His once competent and kind teenage son was disappearing into a delusional world, and it was breaking his heart.

I asked this committed atheist if I could pray. What we were up against was beyond our ability to make a difference.

"Thank you. Please, go ahead."

It was the first of many other times of prayer. Five years later he turned to Jesus and began praying himself.

You could say something like this: "You have been on my heart and I have been praying that you would have strength to endure. Is there anything else I could pray for?"

If the person is open to the idea but nothing comes to mind, you can pray for the following:

- God's comfort (2 Corinthians 1:3)
- his power to help them make it through the next hour (Colossians 1:11)
- power to wait (Psalm 130:5)
- an ability to love other family members (John 15:17)
- confidence that God hears and is near (Psalm 88:1–4; Hebrews 13:6)
- discernment to know where Satan tries to discourage (2 Corinthians 2:11)

Then pray. Pray for the person who stands in front of you. Many of us have never prayed aloud for another person outside of designated prayer times. But praying when face-to-face is a more personal way to bless those we love, and it brings people together, with one mind, before the Lord.

Don't overinterpret grief and suffering.

Human beings prefer to understand causes.

"Why is my computer not working?"
"Why is my child so angry?"
"Why are some people generally happy and others generally sad?"

Care Shaped by Humility

When we or others go through suffering, we want to know why. If we know why, perhaps we can do something about it.

There are, of course, causes for suffering. There are *whys*.

- Adam's sin and the entrance of death
- Our own sin
- The sin of other people
- Satan's afflictions
- God's sovereign will

Yet these causes do not give us the specifics of any one person's suffering. The truth is that there is a mystery in all suffering. We might know why a car is not working, but suffering does not tend to yield to *why* questions. *Why is this happening to me? Why now?* When the suffering person asks these questions, they are more cries for help than cries for answers.

The psalmist cries out, "I say to God, my rock: 'Why have you forgotten me? Why do I go mourning because of the oppression of the enemy?'" (Psalm 42:9). His response? He reminds himself and us of what is most important. "Hope in God; for I shall again praise him, my salvation and my God" (42:11). He is satisfied in that. The details of *why* are not where he looks for comfort. Instead, the psalmist seeks to know God, "that power belongs to God, and that to you, O Lord, belongs steadfast love" (Psalm 62:11–12).

Job, Psalms, and Ecclesiastes are filled with *why* questions. Occasionally God would reveal the obvious to Israel when their blatant idolatry led to their misery, but, more often, the details of *why* are left unanswered. Ecclesiastes, for example, ends with, "fear God and keep his commandments" (Ecclesiastes 12:13). This fear is the potent combination of knowing God's greatness and his love, so we can trust and hope in him alone. The details belong to God.

If there is any cause that we *should not* impose on suffering, unless it is obvious to all, it is our own sin. That was the error of Job's counselors: they assumed that big suffering must have been caused by big sin. It was the mistaken interpretation of blindness. "His [Jesus's] disciples asked him, "Rabbi, who sinned, this man or his parents, that he was born blind?" (John 9:2).

We might think that we would have learned our lesson by the time Jesus himself went through the depths of human suffering. The righteous go through heavy suffering and loss. But we still search for causes, and we still pin them on personal sin. Here you will find the source of many unhelpful comments. In our hubris, we think we know exactly why a person is suffering.

- *Can you think of a time when someone tried to interpret your suffering to you?*

- *What about a time you have tried to do that for someone else?*

- *How does humility change the way you might approach the "why" of suffering?*

Don't start a sentence with "Just . . ."

Our overconfidence might be revealed in the word "just."

"Just pray."
"Just read your Bible."
"Just believe."

"Just" expresses neither compassion nor humility. Compassion listens to what is on the other person's heart; "just" casually tosses out generic bromides. Humility recognizes that suffering is complex in its causes and course; "just" has the answer and knew it before the grieving person spoke a word. Humility also knows that other people have wisdom from which we can learn. "Just" assumes that the other person has somehow forgotten that prayer is a good thing and you need to remind them, or the other person is a child who has not quite learned the rudiments of a godly life. Humility will never come across as demeaning.

When the word "just" is spoken, the consultant has finished the job. A simplistic explanation for a complex problem. Nothing is left to say. People's needs are ignored. This, of course, is not what we expect in God's house. There, God speaks and invites us to respond. We speak from our hearts; he listens and responds. Back and forth. Life with God is participatory and talkative. Though he might speak a word so powerful that it arrests us and causes us to reflect on his words, at some point he anticipates that we will speak to him about those reflections. In human relationships, we follow this pattern whenever we can.

Hold your advice.

"Just" is a specific illustration of how we are prone to act like experts who give advice. Experts do not have to spend time listening because they already know what other people need. Experts may have good intentions—they want to relieve some of the burden of suffering—but they are *self*-confident, and they are wrong on at least two counts. First, experts actually think they can solve and relieve grief. Second, they distance themselves from the grieving person as they assume the role of teacher, which places the grieving person in the role of student.

Advice is, "This is what I think would help (and I know you need it)," or, "This is what I would do if I were you (and I know you need it)." Green tea, a daily jog, a vitamin supplement, a move to another house, a vacation, a pet, etc. These are not necessarily bad ideas, but they leap over both compassion and humility. We haven't asked, "What have *you* found helpful and important?" Perhaps we can give some advice when someone directly asks for it, but even then our respect for their own insights wants to first know what *they* think is wise advice.

If there is one universal rule it is that we don't dispense advice to those who are suffering. What we hope for in our misery is someone who cares, who takes time and is patient, who prays, who enters in and begins to understand. We want a friend who loves, not a consultant who prescribes.

The list of do's and don'ts is growing, and they will be difficult to keep in mind. Remember that these are expressions of compassion and humility. As your lists grow, you will become more skillful in your care for others, but as you grow in humility and love, you will bless them and point them to Jesus.

Accept that you don't know the grieving person completely.

Humility does not pretend to know the reasons and causes of someone's suffering. It also does not claim to know what lies within the grieving person. Even if you have gone through a very similar event, each person's grief is unlike any other. Remember that "Each heart knows its own bitterness" (Proverbs 14:10 NIV). Overconfidence in your knowledge of the person will only lead to further pain for them. Though we *want* to understand, and we work to understand, we can rarely say, "I understand."

It is no surprise that we often ignore this piece of wisdom as we talk with those in our own family. As my father was aging, he shared more of his regrets and struggles with me. Since I thought I knew him well, I assumed there was no reason to ask him for more of his thoughts. Never once did I ask him to help me understand. Never once did I say, "Thank you for sharing your heart with me"—often, "thank you" is an expression of humility. Never did I request, "Please, tell me more." I loved my father, but my self-confidence kept dragging me toward thinking I knew most everything I needed to know. Even when he repeated stories of past regrets, I repeated advice I had already offered. Our relationship was close as he grew old, but that was a result of his love more than my humility.

Offer biblical instruction (and admonition) carefully.

Humility also extends to how we use Scripture. Who could argue with giving Scripture to a grieving person? "Have you been able to hold on to any good words from the Lord?" That is usually a worthy question. It could be followed with, "Let's read Scripture together and listen for them, and let's pray that he will open our ears." Yet the way we bring Scripture can be susceptible to the same problems as giving advice. When Scripture is offered without compassion, and with the assurance that you know what the grieving person needs to hear, it hurts.

Unhelpful instruction might begin with a question:

- "Have you been able to thank and praise God through this?" (The grieving person hears: "You *should*. Maybe that is the real problem.")

- "What is God trying to teach you through this?" (The grieving person hears: "Maybe your problem has to do with sin. The sooner you see it and repent, the quicker you will get through your grief.")

These, of course, are leading questions, which suggest that the grieving person is spiritually lacking and not in sync with the Spirit. These implicit admonitions put new burdens on the hurting person, and unless we realize it and ask for forgiveness, our relationship will be damaged.

Let's take the questions one at a time.

> "Have you been able to thank and praise God through this?"

Scripture does say we are to give "thanks always and for everything" (Ephesians 5:20). Praise and thanks are, indeed, to flow from the heart of God's children. We are thankful to God, who in Jesus Christ fully revealed his love and faithfulness to unfaithful people. We are also thankful for the many expressions of life that flow from his continued presence with us and in this world. This extends to provisions for daily life and the beauty of creation. But there are things we are *not* called to be thankful for: sin, Satan, death, violence, victimization, other forms of injustice, and all kinds of evil. Following our

Father's lead, we make judgments and rightly decide that some things are decidedly *not* good, and giving thanks for them would be ungodly.

Scripture also says, there is "a time for every matter under heaven" (Ecclesiastes 3:1). Times of mourning are not when we encourage someone to look on the bright side and give thanks and praise to God. Indeed, Proverbs argues the opposite: "Whoever sings songs to a heavy heart is like one who takes off a garment on a cold day" (Proverbs 25:20). Grief is a time to lament with the sufferer, and the psalms of lament can guide us.[4] These psalms mark times when we pour out our heart to the Lord, as this writer did when he described the grief of Jewish exiles.

> By the waters of Babylon,
>> there we sat down and wept,
>> when we remembered Zion.
> On the willows there
>> we hung up our lyres.
> For there our captors
>> required of us songs,
> and our tormentors, mirth, saying,
>> "Sing us one of the songs of Zion!"
>>> (Psalm 137:1–3)

Mourning is the order of the day in these psalms, and this mourning is the will of God. It reflects his own heart as he too waits for the day when mourning will end for his people.

The second inappropriate question—

"What is God trying to teach you?"

—is in the style of Job's comforters. It makes a connection between someone's suffering and specific sin. It assumes that there is something amiss to which the person is blind, and God needs to bring out the big guns so they will get the message. But Job's friends were wrong about the reason for Job's suffering, and God rebuked them for it (Job 42:7–8).

The New Testament goes on to suggest a very different reason for suffering. With the Old Testament, it agrees that suffering is the lot of humanity until Jesus returns. But Jesus changes everything now. God brings his people on the *Via Dolorosa*, making suffering an element of our union with Christ and participation in his life and death (Philippians 1:29). And yes, "We know that in all things God works for the good of those who love him" (Romans 8:28 NIV), but a person's suffering is not a riddle to be solved so we can discern the specifics of God's sovereign will. And the good that unfolds from suffering takes a lifetime to see.

Of course, it is not contrary to humility to bring Scripture to a person who grieves. Scripture, after all, is the very word of life to our souls. Instead, humility asks the grieving person questions like the following:

"Do you have a favorite Scripture?"

"Has there been any passage that has strengthened you?"

"Is there a particular Scripture we could read together?"

"Could I read a verse to you that I read this morning that helped my heart?"

Questions like these enter through the portals of compassion and humility. When you bring Scripture in this way, you could paraphrase Augustine: Love God, proceed with love and humility, and read whatever Scripture you please.

Here is an example:

A woman was sitting in the hospital room of her elderly mother whose death seemed close. She asked her, "Do you believe that to die is gain?" She was echoing the apostle Paul's words, "For me, to live is Christ, and to die is gain" (Philippians 1:21 NIV). That question was at the crossroads of implicit accusation and humility with compassion. One path says, "No, you probably don't believe this right now"; the other says, "The words of Paul are so important, let's consider them together." At that moment, in which humble love and compassion were standard fare in the relationship, the mother never detected a hint of accusation. She heard words from her daughter that fixed her on spiritual reality and invited a response that kept her occupied for the next day, after which she responded with a smile, "Yes, I do believe that." The words from her daughter were perfect.

As we build our wisdom in pastoral care, we need to remember that being biblically correct is not enough. "Right" words have been spoken by Pharisees, Job's comforters, and demons. Compassion doesn't settle for being right.

Compassion asks, Do my words satisfy the law of love?

Humility adds: Are you willing to ask the person how you could come to Scripture together? Do you assume that you have the divine interpretation of the person's hardships? Do you live under Scripture and need to hear its words, or do you dispense it? Do you understand the Scripture you use?

These qualifications are important, but you can't go wrong when you love the person and say, "Let me read some Scripture." And then read. Where else can we turn and find words of life? Grieving people can be too exhausted to think and not have words to say, but hearing Scripture from a friend can be a unique comfort.

Be cautious as you respond to theological questions.

Over time, you might hear questions such as, "Why did God do this? Why is he silent?"

These questions seem to have answers in Scripture. For example, a person says, "This is more than I can bear." Scripture responds, "He will . . . provide a way out so that you can endure it" (1 Corinthians

10:13 NIV). Wise care seems obvious. The person asked a direct question and you give a direct answer.

Still, as a general rule, *don't* answer theological questions until you understand more about the question. Some questions are burdens to be shared. They are rhetorical, and the person is not asking for an answer. Other questions are personal questions in disguise.

"Can people who commit suicide go to heaven?"

The obvious response is, "Tell me more about why you are thinking about suicide?" The person might be thinking about a friend, in which the real matter is how to help. Or the question is even more personal. The person asking is thinking about suicide.

The questions that chronic sufferers have about God are often personal. They feel abandoned and punished. Their words are cries from their heart, and their questions are rhetorical. To launch into an answer is to violate compassion that desires to know the person, and it violates humility if you think you actually have the answer before even understanding the person's true concern.

Humility could lead you in this way: "Please tell me more." "Have you been able to speak these questions to the Lord?" This could be followed by reading together parts of Psalm 22.

> My God, my God, why have you forsaken me? Why are you so far from

> saving me, from the words of my groaning? O my God, I cry by day, but you do not answer, and by night, but I find no rest. (22:1–2).

Then you could pray the words that the Spirit must affix to the heart.

> He has not despised or abhorred the affliction of the afflicted, and he has not hidden his face from him, but has heard, when he cried to him. (22:24)

Pray with them.

When humility meets love, we pray. Grief and loss are meant to be spoken to God. At first, you might pray on behalf of the other person. That is the honor called intercessory prayer. You pray what the other person has spoken to you. You gather in a promise of God, such as how he "comforts us in all our affliction" (2 Corinthians 1:4). Then you ask if the grieving person would pray with you. While grieving, this, of course, is much more difficult than it seems. We can speak *about* God easier than we speak *to* him. If speaking to the Lord has been hard for them, invite them to speak to God with you. Praying together with those who grieve may be the most important means of care you can offer. It is God's desire for us to come to him in this way.

> Pour out your hearts to him.
> (Psalm 62:8 NIV)

> The Lord's hand is not shortened, that it cannot save, or his ear dull, that it cannot hear. (Isaiah 59:1)

> He who planted the ear, does he not hear? (Psalm 94:9)

God invites us to ask him the hard and painful questions on our hearts. "Why, O Lord, do you stand far away?" (Psalm 10:1). He hears our cries and is our only true refuge.

We know we are on the right path when, together, we speak to the Lord. With practice, we can come to him, with confidence, even boldness. "O Lord, hear my voice! Let your ears be attentive to the voice of my pleas for mercy!" (Psalm 130:2).

LEARNERS FOR LIFE

What might you add to these lists? One of the pleasures of life in Christ is that the more we grow in wisdom and care for others, the more we desire to grow. There will never come a time when we think we have mastered compassion and humility and can move on to the next topic.

I recently learned from a friend whose wife received very difficult news after a routine medical exam. He said to the physician, "Thank you for being honest and clear. We're not looking to you for comfort, only truth. We look to Jesus for comfort." This encouraged my own confidence in Jesus, and it has already caused me to pray more persistently that those I care for will know the comfort of Jesus.

As learners, we will still toss out platitudes like "God is in control," but maybe this time we will apologize for speaking without caring. Then compassion and humility take over.

> "I have been thinking about rest and how in suffering it seems like there is no rest. In Psalm 55 the psalmist wonders if rest can only come if he flies away. Do you think it would be helpful to read Scripture that reminds us that God is much greater and closer than we know?"

> "Here is part of a psalm that caused me to pray for you. I'll read it to you and you can tell me what you think. It is about how God is faithful and over everything, so we can trust him."

Imagine. Compassion that even the suffering person can see. Humility that walks *with* the person, even coming under the person. You can probably remember right now someone who extended humble compassion to you. Some things are too beautiful and spiritual to be forgotten.

Imagine a church—and a group of friends, and a family—that cares for suffering and grieving people in a way that builds up and brings together, in a way that the compassion, gentleness, and humility of Jesus are on display.

Let's say a friend confides in you about lingering depression or fears that have taken hold. The request has an effect on you. Your friend is being more vulnerable and open compared to "Could you pray that I would get an A on Monday's test?" You, in turn, are blessed that you were found worthy to receive this fine china of the heart, and you pray. You pray, you remember, and you want to know your friend even more. As your friend is encouraged by your care, that person is more alert to the burdens of other people and prays, remembers, and knows them more deeply. Meanwhile, you also might be inspired to be more open with your own struggles, and you ask for prayer . . . and the body of Christ becomes more attractive.

That is the opportunity and privilege before us.

RESOURCES

1. Your primary resource is those who are grieving and those who have grieved. They are your experts. Ask people to tell their stories. How were they affected by a loss? How does it affect them now? Did they find direction and comfort in Scripture? Were particular passages important? What words and actions from friends were most helpful and least helpful? If others are willing to speak these gifts to you, humility will say "thank you," and compassion will pray.

2. Nancy Guthrie has written a useful book on how to pray Scripture for those who grieve. *I'm Praying for You: 40 Days of Praying the Bible for Someone Who Is Suffering* (10Publishing, 2021). Nancy has also compiled a series of devotionals written by saints past and

present (Keller, Yancey, Bonhoeffer, Spurgeon, Newton), *Be Still, My Soul: Embracing God's Purpose and Provision in Suffering* (Crossway, 2010). These could be read with a grieving person and become occasions for important conversations.

3. Mark Vroegop has taken seriously the task of crying out to the Lord. One of his books on lament is *Dark Clouds, Deep Mercy: Discovering the Grace of Lament* (Crossway, 2019).

4. Joni Eareckson Tada has written many fine books on suffering. You could pick up any of them and find something true and helpful. One that is dense with important teaching and followed by a helpful list of Scripture is *When God Weeps: Why Our Sufferings Matter to the Almighty* (Zondervan, 2000).

ENDNOTES

1. Robert H. Gundry, *Commentary on the New Testament* (Peabody, MA: Hendrickson, 2010), 635.

2. A false but common assumption (based on Ephesians 5:20) that Christians are to be thankful in all things. More on this later.

3. Nancy Guthrie, *What Grieving People Wish You Knew about What Really Helps (and What Really Hurts)* (Wheaton, IL: Crossway, 2016).

4. For example you might read lament Psalms such as Psalms 3, 5, 10, 22, 27, 51, and 64. You also might find helpful Mark Vroegop's book *Dark Clouds, Deep Mercy: Discovering the Grace of Lament* (Wheaton, IL: Crossway, 2019).

ASK THE CHRISTIAN COUNSELOR

The Ask the Christian Counselor series from New Growth Press is a series of compact books featuring biblical counseling answers to many of life's common problems. This series walks readers through their deepest and most profound questions. Each question is unpacked by an experienced counselor, who gives readers the tools to understand their struggle and to see how the gospel brings hope and healing to the problem they are facing.

Each book in the series is longer than our popular minibooks, but still short enough not to overwhelm the reader. These books can be read by individuals on their own or used within a counseling setting.

NewGrowthPress.com